Remote Life

EDWARD ANKI

BareBackPress

BareBackPress
Hamilton, Ontario, Canada
For enquires visit www.barebackpress.com
For information contact press@barebacklit.com
Cover layout and art: © Choi Yunnam

POEMS

For Uncle Mike

Remote
Life

Age Eight

One of the bad guys
became a good guy
and teamed up with a good guy
to fight two bad guys
and the two good guys
beat the two bad guys
and that was very exciting.

After the match
the good guy
(formerly a bad guy)
sucker-punched his teammate
and the two bad guys
they had beaten
returned to the wrestling ring
and helped the good guy
(now once again a bad guy)
stomp and kick the good guy
and that was very sad.

Two other good guys
(formerly bad guys)
saw what was happening
and jumped into the action
and overpowered all three bad guys
and helped the fallen good guy
to his feet.

"Lunch is ready," my mother called.

I walked into the dining room,
prepared for the world.

Wrong Direction

She slurred her words
and made ignorant comments
about the cabbie's turban and
I thought I ought
to boot her ass out of this vehicle
treat the cabbie to a beer
delete my online dating profile
fly to Japan
enter a monastery
relinquish booze
and women
and television
and everything which has brought me
to where I am
now paying this cabbie
entering her apartment
and saying
nice place
you got here.

Remote Life

The game shows
the talk shows
the sitcoms
the reality shows
the sluggish eyes
of apparent lovers
on nightmarishly calm
Sunday evenings.

To think:

Decades before
these were children
STAMPING
their feet into puddles
with joyous abandon.

Now
one of them
reaches out,
changes the channel.

The coffins yawn
in anticipation.

Tunnel Vision

Terrible things are happening to very good people
right now.

A tube up the ass
a breast removed
bandages ripped from burned skin.

And that's in civilized parts.

In other parts of the world
and perhaps in dark corners
of these parts
testicles are being shocked
fingernails pulled
faces being pushed into
puddles of self-made
urine.

Meanwhile I sit
up in bed
miserable.

Work
tomorrow,
again.

Scenic View

The strip joint goes mostly unnoticed
at the corner of Dirtball Drive and Weary Way
as do the rooms above
with their filthy curtains their memories
of so much sad sawdust indifference in the eyes
of the poster girls pinned to the walls.

Now a pigeon lands on the windowsill
a man hunches on the bed edge
a woman spreads herself to the vastness
of the smallness of the moment and
the pigeon flies away.

Christmas Eve

The children of everywhere
lay out their cookies
and dream up colorful gods and gifts
and now *Anastasia* takes the stage
wrapping the pole
with her body
for six separately seated men
aged thirty-seven to
sixty-three.

Sanity

I've tried straight win bets
bets across the board
boxing horses wheeling them
the daily doubles
the pick-3's
the win-4's

I've tried picking horses based on time
class
previous wins
jockeys
trainers
head to head match-ups with other horses
the way a horse's ass
shakes in the wind.

I've tried betting sober
drunk
at peace
disgruntled
employed
the other way around
and back again.

But I'm done
trying.

I have won money at most one in every ten times that I've
been out
to the racetrack and tonight,
finally and quietly,
in the privacy of my small apartment
the door locked
the music gentle and easy

I have gratefully given up.

Beating the horses is almost, if not actually, impossible.
The odds are too short!
Or too long!

Just looking at those guys in there tonight,
mostly old, so sad and angry,
pants too short, jackets worn with the grief of too many
winters
just looking at those guys in there tonight
that's all the proof that any sane person needs.

It's taken me nearly fifteen years
to become sane.

To realize that the only way to make money is
sports or dice or cards.

Anything but work.

Only the truly insane go that route.

Betty

She's been working in the clubhouse
for decades,
although initially
she served in one
of the grandstand bars.

Now,
nearing retirement,
she hobbles on calloused feet
from table to table,
taking orders and delivering food and drink
amidst the shouts of patrons,
most of them men,
some of whom
she has been serving for several years.

The afternoons wear on,
race after race
from tracks across the continent
unfolding on the television screens
occupying one entire side of the restaurant,
the cigar smoke growing thicker,
the losing tickets
accumulating on the tables,
the hollers and the shouts
becoming increasingly
desperate
savage
crazed
while outside,
in a world easily forgotten,
the sun slowly gives way
to inevitable dusk.

And then Betty is on her way home,
and then she is home,
back in that tidy little apartment
where for years
she has been living
with well dusted photographs of her long dead husband.

Another day gone,
another night alone
but for the echoes of fools.

Fortune
never lasts.

Shift's End

The end arrived
in the autumn of his 61st year,
three days
after walking home from the racetrack,
gripped with chest pain,
his pill-head wife
rousing herself from the tattered couch
to call the ambulance.

The end had arrived –
or so it seemed to him
during his final few days –
soon after the beginning had begun.
Running along winding cobblestone streets
in a small Italian village
one moment,
wheeled into ICU
the next.

"A dream,"
he muttered,
shortly before he died.

The nurse
checked her watch.

Disposable

Three floors down
footprints
in the snow
mark the journey
from the back entrance
to a tattered floral print couch
next to a garbage dumpster
at the rear of the building.

I look again.
Did the couch
just shrug?

I do the same.

Score

It was a great date
sitting there beneath green barroom light
making it work making it happen
a great date so little to say
so much being said.

Her name was Emily
or Sandra
or Cassandra
or Slippery Sue
or something hard to remember
so long ago now
thinking back to last night
in that green bar
with Sideways Sarah.

Afterwards we took a taxi back to her place and her mutt
was on the bed and she cooed and frolicked
with her mutt
and they made baby faces at each other
and the mutt licked her nose
and I poured a drink
and looked out the living room window
and thought
I'm getting older
what the fuck am I doing here
what the fuck am I doing here?

And afterwards it was afterwards
on my back in her bed
and I still didn't know.

Incomplete

So many singles
searching
for some apparent
soulmate
in so many ways –
online
in bars
in soup kitchens
supermarkets
along the boardwalk
in volleyball leagues
on streetcars
during lunch break
at work
so many singles
searching
for completion
in somebody else.

The married
searching
elsewhere . . .

For the same thing.

Morning Song

Up into my eyes
she smiled
while I did my moaning and groaning routine
which is not a routine
in the sense of being artificial
just a routine in the sense of being
routine like death is routine
or shopping or shitting or sitting
through bad Sunday night movies
or anything at all that happens
over and over again
without too much variation
can be routine although
I would hardly describe the act of ejaculation
as routine not ever
and especially not this morning
smiling into her eyes
while the bedsprings sang
of the moment
passing.

Noise

I walked in through
the back door and
passed one of the kitchen guys
going the other way
for a cigarette.

What's up I asked?
How's it going?
he nodded back.

In the change room
one of the waiters was
tightening the noose
on his tie.

What's going on?
How you been?
I responded.

Behind the bar
I greeted the daytime
bartender with a hearty
handshake.

How's it hanging?
Loose and full of juice!
I told him.

Eight hours later
I was back
in my apartment
drinking a beer.

An entire day

without speaking
to a single person.

I tried the
TV.

Vacation

It was a family of four from Pittsburgh
and I liked them straight away.

The daughter was cross-eyed with a seeming dent in her
forehead
the son was grossly overweight
the mother
also a porker
had a bit of a moustache
and the father
besides being obviously miserable
was wearing a faded white Pittsburgh Penguins t-shirt.

They sat at the bar and asked me to put on the hockey game.
The Penguins were in the Stanley Cup finals.

The mother drank two draught beers
the father consumed two glasses of wine
the kids loaded up on water
all of them ordered pasta
and the Penguins got shut out by Detroit for the second game
in a row.

Eventually, the father got up and walked out of the bar.

He's miserable the mother told me.
I nodded.
He's been miserable the whole trip
the hideous daughter confirmed.
More water I asked?
Sure she answered.

What a welcome relief that family was
what a break from the rich and stylish urbanites

who feel the need to modify every dish
or the business men who can barely
find the time to look up at me while ordering.

Such blessed creatures
chomping at their food
repeatedly emptying the bread basket
slurping and gulping their drinks.

A breath of fresh manure
in a world of perfumed
death.

Death Row

Inside the nursing home
they lounge in the lobby
addled beneath the
strong yellow light
some in wheelchairs
others on hard plastic seats
they sit and sit and sit
rarely speaking moving only
to perhaps scratch an
ass or pick a nose.

They have arrived from
everywhere and now they
stare out through the lobby window
their medicated brains noting
the falling snow
the passing automobiles
the people walking by
those residents just sit and sit and sit
as screaming babies are born
as coffins are sanded smooth
as fresh dirt is packed
into the cold hard ground
the dinky Christmas lights
adorning the lobby window
blinking lethargically on
and then off
each successive repetition
bringing Christmas Day closer
to be followed by
New Year's Eve
to be followed by
another cold January
soggy with grey skies.

The holiday season has arrived
and while for some residents
Christmas may never again
arrive they are at least
enjoying the festivities
while they can.

Scratching their asses and
picking their noses
while unfortunate others
worry about
death.

The Driftwood Inn

An old man,
he walks,
up the stairs.

Room #203.
He enters . . .
The room is decent,
no dead bodies,
television where it should be,
bed where it should be,
bathroom where it should be.

He removes his jacket,
his shoes,
reaches for the remote.

Two guys talking about football.
Next channel.
A prayer line.
Next channel . . .

He decides against watching television,
showers,
settles into bed.

He'll check his lottery ticket
in the morning.

Ache

Another Sunday night visit
complete
I hug my mother
and say goodnight.

It's always somewhat sad,
departing,
watching that door close
one more time,
walking towards the bus stop
as she settles
into her bungalow
alone.

How did this moment arrive?
My mother, a senior citizen!
Myself, a middle aged man!

It's such a blur . . .
all the births
and deaths
and Christmases
and Easters
and birthdays
and now,
already,
the first bite of autumn in the air.

My girlfriend greets me
with a smile
as I walk through the doorway.

"How was your visit with your mom?"
"It was good," I respond,

leaving the unexplainable
unexpressed.

The Night Before I Dumped Her

Her dog approached
the couch
while I was responding to her
question regarding the benefits
of meditation.

Winston! she exclaimed,
turning towards the mutt,
you're so cute!

I stopped talking.

Go ahead,
she said,
I'm listening.

She was still
looking
at her
dog.

Reunion

Five weeks after
I dumped her
I was on top,
beads of sweat
from my forehead
dripping down onto
her breasts.

Later –
while I seasoned the meat –
she paused
over a cucumber.

"Do you really love me?"

"Of course,"
I guessed,
assuredly.

She brought
the knife
down.

Nostalgia

Too much soreness in the region around the heart
and a steady ache between the scalp
and the soles of the feet everything headache sunlight
now everything hardly anything it once was.

An Aging Bachelor

Putting on your shoes,
doing up your shoelaces,
locking your front door.

Starting your car,
buckling your seatbelt,
weaving through traffic.

Filling out a form,
sitting in the emergency waiting room.

Your name is finally called,
you explain the problem,
pissing blood.

The doctor is young,
he tells you to undress.

Maybe
you should have married.

One Curtain Over

He lays there
night after night
shitting his brains
out.

Bedpan,
he groans,
bedpan.

It's always a big mess.
Sometimes he even
shits in his sleep.
Loud crackles and pops
emanating
from his cheeks.

The nurses,
little Filipino ladies,
wipe his ass for him,
prepare the sheets
and bedpan
for his next episode.

Evaporation

For nearly two decades
she frequented the same small diner
several times a week,
often for lunch and sometimes for breakfast,
the waitresses knew her,
the cooks knew her,
even the handful of old drunks
who guzzled cheap draft at the bar
knew her,
through wind rain sleet snow
she arrived
after walking the three blocks
from her modest one-bedroom apartment.

It wasn't much,
naturally,
but it was something,
some place to go for hot coffee,
for eggs and toast or a sandwich,
for a few simple words,
for a nod,
for an occasionally genuine smile.

Several days after she'd followed
the lead
of her long dead husband
word leaked slowly through the diner,
sighs were exchanged,
the old Italian owner
even snuck a shot of brandy,
steadied himself
amidst the evaporating
years . . .

The following day
was complete with clanking plates,
incoming orders,
and outgoing
memories.

Southbound

Observing human beings
on the subway
at eight o'clock
on a weekday morning
it becomes easy to believe
hell has arrived.

Sour mouths
downcast eyes
fidgety fingers searching for distraction
in blackberries or cell phones or discarded newspapers
or anything at all.

Suddenly an old woman,
quite obviously a vagabond,
unzips her pants
pulls her faded purple underwear
down to her ankles
and assuming a full squat
begins to piss
a splashing stream
onto the train floor.

I watch from a safe distance
as those in her immediate vicinity
become very alert
very fast
clearing space
for the apparent lunatic.

Finally finished,
the old woman
pulls up her pants
and then,

as if nothing had happened,
exits at the next stop.

The train moves forward
and the buzzing of voices
begins.

What a nut!
What a crazy old bitch!
Holy shit!
What the hell?

I simply watch
the piss,
slowly crawling
south.

December 31st

You shut the light,
crawl into bed,
stare up
into the darkness.

They're out there tonight:
fat bodies thin bodies short bodies
tall bodies
bodies crammed together
in clubs
at house parties
bodies roaming the streets
screaming bodies singing bodies
laughing crying puking
bodies
pounding the very Earth
while you wonder
how many years
you might have left.

The thought is frightening,
nonetheless
pausing to think
feels warranted
as the seconds tick
down.

Acknowledgements:

Some of the poems in this collection first appeared or will appear in *Jobbers*, *Qwerty*, *The Chaffin Journal*, *Plain Spoke*, *Mad Poets Review*, and *Left Behind: A Journal of "Shock" Literature*. Thanks to the editors of these journals and magazines. Thanks as well to Damon Ferrell Marbut for suggesting revisions to some of these poems.

About the Author:

Edward Anki currently resides in Toronto, Canada. This is his first published collection of poetry.